PRAIRIE FEVER

D0815168

PRAIRIE FEVER

MARY BIDDINGER

Mary Biddinger

BOWLING GREEN, KENTUCKY

9/7/07
For Varley,
with a warm
welcome to
Northeast Ohio!
It's wonderful to
have you here.
Fondly,
Mary B.

Book Design by Jill Ihasz
Cover Design by C. L. Knight
Author and cover photographs: Gregory Thompson

Steel Toe Books
Department of English
135 Cherry Hall
Western Kentucky University
1 Big Red Way
Bowling Green, KY 42101-3576
www.steeltoebooks.com

TABLE OF CONTENTS

ACKNOWLEDGEMENTS

Grateful acknowledgement is made to the editors of the following magazines in which these poems first appeared, sometimes in slightly different versions:

ACM: Fish in Winter, Salsa at the Belair Lounge
American Literary Review: Man in Blue
Apalachee Review: Show Pony, Velvet Season
The Bedside Guide to No Tell Motel: Copper Harbor
Bluesky Review: A Western, Coyote
The Briar Cliff Review: Dogs in the Woods
Crazyhorse: Drift
The Eleventh Muse: Snakeskin
Fourteen Hills: Dirndl in a Tree
Good Foot: Wheatfield Shag, A Ghazal
Harpur Palate: It's All Too Much
Hobble Creek Review: The Edge of Town, Ferns
Indiana Review: The Rookery
The Iowa Review: Brick Dust
The Journal: Slim
Notre Dame Review: Two
Pavement Saw: Commonlaw
Perihelion: Bird Bones
Plainsongs: Housewarming
Ploughshares: Razorback
Portland Review: Manistee
Puerto del Sol: Anklebone
Red Rock Review: Bird of Danger
Salt Hill: Driving Away from Your Body, The Flyers
Seven Corners: Foxgloves at 3 pm, Milfoil & Afterthought,
    Red Sea, Royal Blue, The Twins

Spoon River Poetry Review: Lunar Eclipse
Stray Dog: Kicking It
Sycamore Review: Girl in Chair

I wish to thank the Chicago Union League Civic and Arts
Foundation, Illinois Arts Council, and Ragdale Foundation
for fellowships and awards that helped me complete this
work. Thanks to the University of Illinois at Chicago and The
University of Akron for helping support my teaching, writing,
and scholarship.

Sincere gratitude to the friends, editors, and advisors who
helped this book become what it is today: Michael Anania,
Nin Andrews, Robert Archambeau, Dale Barrigar, Mackenzie
Carignan, Brent Fisk, Elton Glaser, Brandi Homan, Tom C.
Hunley, Simone Muench, Aimee Nezhukumatathil, Sterling
Plumpp, Bob Pope, Jackie White, and Anne Winters.

For their excellent moral and poetic support, thank you to
the Akron Poetry Collective, Chicago Women's Poetry Group,
ladies of the Juniverse, and my dear friends at RHINO.

Thanks to my family for their patience and faith: Greg,
Gabriella, and Raymond, and my parents, Patsy and Scott
Biddinger.

For Gabi and Ray

I.

BENEATH THE TRACKS

SALSA AT THE BELAIR LOUNGE ✓

Even Roy Orbison
would get lost
in my hair. I shake it:
doorframe, jukebox,
tongues, domino

sugar bag. A lime
to bite instead of your
finger. The mango skirt,
snagged silk, crinoline.
You can't dance.

I leave a hand print
on the wall in grenadine.
My shoes are new, cork
heels, like fifteen years
ago. A woman crosses

the room for a smoke.
She knows my song
even in buckskin boots.
Black doily, goldleaf
teeth, sea salt, avocado

halves in the freezer.
I'm with Mamà, washing
tumblers again. Pouring
a steamed glass of beer
down my back. No,

I am dancing, losing
my skirt to your hands.
Snakeskin. The record
is over. All aprons off
and hot like bleeding.

THE FLYERS ✓

The blue lights of an Ohio airfield
are the hundred eyes of a peacock
tail. Across the tracks, one cracked

windowpane with a honeydew melon
on the sill, as if waiting for sunrise.
Leaf bins on the curb, green bottles

crushed under Chevy tires. Walk me
through this once again. There are
houses the size of my kitchen, white,

leaning as if people lined the walls,
fell backwards until the eaves listed.
Tell me the story of the woman lost

down a stone well for weeks before
they noticed the laundry wasn't done.
How we saw her ironing yellow pleats

beside a backyard wash tub, chicken
feathers scattered beneath the bushes.
Her daughter sick from crabapples,

or was it the well water we shared
with all of them, held up in Ball jars
for examination. Underneath elms

and creepers, a tow truck shudders
into late shift. Its carnival tail lights
are cherries pickled in gin and salt.

Show me all the turns to the field
of broken glass and pachysandras,
women easing out of back seats

and into twisting cigarillo smoke
at midnight. What species of Cessna
crosses these rooftops, loops above

mildewed steeples and the backside
of parables, to the crow holes, gnats,
slow drip of a hose left in knots.

DRIFT

What you did that day
beneath the tracks

and zigzag of crab grass,
coneflowers bending.

This, you said, *prairie
fever.* How the canal

worked you to buckshot.
A woman in an upstairs

window behind drapes.
Gravel elevator slick

below the thunderheads.
Your brother ransacked

every jar in search of keys
or maps. It took a year

for you to dig your way
to water. Maroon velour

of blood on your cheek.
A waitress offering cobbler

and a phone to authorities.
Pheasants connecting field

and table. It was rhubarb.
The sheets were polyester

satin. Bottlebrush, silky wild
rye, or your own tangled hair

underwater. The way it all
went down. Cyclones of rope,

flashlights, coriander skin.
The smoke from downriver.

DOGS IN THE WOODS

Your story had a wool blanket,
two naked men, Mell's trestle,
Shalimar. We were just girls
in the sheep stalls, dirt biking
uptown in braids and gloss.

My mother dusted the ashtray
for your mother's afternoon
cigarette. By school we watched
the boat launch in aprons, snips
of dandelion, someone at your
neck, always. Like the rhubarb

pies you ate with your hands
in the field behind Central
after they slipped. Blue jays
snatched the crust right in front
of us, flapped away with lipstick
cheeks. I wore my French lace

dress and walked the drive-in
alone. Borrowed your garters,
a man who looked forty and drove
an Impala like guns were out.
There was this place they called
nothing, but you'd been there.

I'm *Shane*. My name would be
Holly, or anything rougher
than my own thigh and undershirt.
I *have a friend who done things.*
My scarf was candy stripe
orange. The sour kind that lasts
all day whether you want it or not.

THE EDGE OF TOWN

Girls walked the tracks
in terrycloth halters, lingered
around concrete blocks jutting
through the reeds. The horizon:

shattered windows of a high rise
like the quivering squares of water
left when I pressed my tongue
against a screen door. Fourteen

and too old to ride a three-speed
along the river bed. Freight cars
carried the men south, stalled
at intersections for hours while

the girls smoked Parliaments
under a cloak of citronella.
I soaked my hands every night
but refused to rinse my hair

in beer like they did, fingers
on the pull-tab and heads upside
down in the shower. Sometimes
they would tag the rail cars

in spray paint: *foxy* or *wash me*
or hearts and daggers. We pasted
leaves and wrappers on our bodies
with spit, ate our lunches squatting

in the clearing, matches ready
for ticks. When three men drifted
down the river on their backs
we looked to the trees. A grackle

landed on one man's naked
stomach, began preening. Trout
churned in the shallows as he
pinwheeled through the cattails

like a windmill with white eyes.
You could still see tobacco spit
on his chin, a wristband of black
electrical tape under waterlogged

flannel. We used branches to push
him until the river took over.
I saw him for years after that day:
behind the wheel of an ice truck,

in a conductor's hat and coveralls.
Lurking in the stalls of the farmer's
market, iridescent behind corn silk.
Across the hospital waiting room,

hand wrapped in a green gingham
curtain. Beneath a wool army blanket
in my bed, in damp spaces between
my back and the hardwood floor.

[DIRNDL IN A TREE]

WILD
POEMS

Yard flecked with trillium
like private school collars
spread open on green
and ochre. The buzz

saw made its false wasp
drone, and no one heard
my footsteps on the cedar

chips. His hand around
my waist, mouth on my
earlobe. Calluses, stain
all the way to his wrists.

That damn bird in his bed,
then on the kitchen table,
the workbench, hearth,

upside down in the attic,
between his skinny thighs
on the roof. Like the wall
of flying ants that fizzed

for days on my old house.
Face in Beulah's starchy
armpit as mother sprayed

the gasoline. It all went
up, but the sound left us
quiet in smoke, wings.
Everything stops at noon

13

with the soup bell, except
my man already sucking
his tin of boiled hog bones.

He could have been my
brother, except he was old
and naked under coveralls.
Flecks of maple fell from

his hair down to the tree.
Squeezing his thumb, I
saw the second the skin

burst into blood. My two
legs seemed too far apart,
running away. Things went
under and through me, like

stumps, piles of wet grass,
a biting pony, other men.

A GHAZAL

Nights we read the paper and ate oranges.
Wrapped peel and damp thighs in newsprint.

(The person who taught you to bathe in pants
could solder the wings back on a grasshopper.)

You were so beautiful, I took the night ferry
with grease and beards of young subway men.

The lady next door made wine in a pole barn.
Daffodils flipped inside out, finches up my ears.

Naked in the burned-down house. Snow falling
through the roof, a disco ball in the rafters.

The ghost movie of headlights on bed sheets
brought me back to thirteen, and blue rock sugar.

Crouched along a turnpike at midnight, skunks
painted wild lanes with white dash backs.

When you found my silver shoe in the hedges:
heel slick against your porchlit tongue.

Not sure where I was headed without my keys,
but I rode you two hundred miles anyway.

ANKLEBONE √

Some towns have the story
of a man gone mad.
Our town had the dead girl.
How I wanted to be her.

> *A wreath of ants*
> *belly-up in the bath.*
> *Clothes that once smelled*
> *precisely of doughnuts.*
> *The amber leaf*
> *her lipstick left*
> *on everything she touched.*

I learned to be her
in the turquoise motel
when I woke to deer prints
on the carpet, a door
just recently shut.

Some chose to revise her.
Gave her a saint's middle name,
a derelict uncle back from Texas,
or even the stigmata
(which no one could picture).

> *A book sunk to the bottom*
> *of the tub. Her terrycloth robe*
> *still folded. A yellow bulb*
> *and halo of dried moths*
> *her mother swept into a bag.*

I learned to be her
on my sixteenth birthday.
A friend poisoned one piece
of the cake. We all ate
but I did not die.

An old woman once claimed
to see her perched
in the eves of the rectory.
But nothing was found
when they brought in the dogs.

  Sheers soaked to the rod
  with bathwater. No soap.
  Her hair ribbon's dye
  bleeding onto ceramic.
  A shower curtain torn
  from its hooks.

I learned to be her
the day I floated downstream
on my back. The river
filled my mouth and ears
and I drifted out of town.

THE ROOKERY

CROWS

Once I was stolen
by a man and woman
who wanted me as their own.

Crows do not dive
into captive water, as I dove
the day I was taken
from Santa Fe, from a drunken
party by a hotel pool.
The task was simple.
I was seven, and promised
a yard full of mule deer
gentle as dogs.

What I got was Arizona,
three to a mattress,
a glass of creamer and pretzel
for breakfast. Strange
how cold the desert grows
past sunset, with the rumble
of wolves and weary daybirds.

But crows adjust to the terrain
they're given. In other countries
they're *jackdaws* or *rooks*;
some call them blackbirds,
a name reminding me of berries.
Blackbird. Beneath the briars
you will find your fruit,

and under the hovering crow
circle a steer's head, picked
clean. The man and woman slept
naked, and I in the middle.
Day became the night

and I was cold in both. Cold
on lambskin car seats, scanning
the radio and learning to smoke
the woman's True Blues, to sit
still while my hair was braided.

Then one day I lay
in a dustlot by the interstate
and watched. It took hours
for the first bird to appear.
The third I trapped beneath
my hair. The third I rapped
with a stone and broke.

SHOW PONY

Every year the fair came
they let the rhinoceros out
to see if he'd come back.

Boxes of tiny panda
mice, bags of goldfish
and other small prizes.
The girl with the heart
grown outside her body
stayed at the Ramada
for safe-keeping.

In the exhibit hall
ten rows of berry pies,
and that woman who grew
earwigs a finger's length
on a diet of cornstarch
and ground turkey.

The girl with her heart
played cards in the grotto.
I threw fried dough at her
because she was not
lovely, but still caught
every eye. Hourly
she'd unbutton.

The boy raised by
wolves watched harness
racing, greased pig
chases. The heart girl
loved him, but he loved
everyone, and was also
known to bite.

When the rhino arrived,
the concert was underway.
Trophy hunters followed
him closely. The earwigs
left their meal piles
and shuttled up walls.

Should we be happy
our paths crossed
so many times?
The heart girl wept
in the bandstand
as goldfish circled
their plastic bags.

WHEATFIELD SHAG

My sister's hair was the shade
of onion skins, or wallpaper
in a flooded house. Veins

grape hyacinth under puff
sleeves, tulle and twirl, slip
clung to thighs, electric.

Trace of nosebleed down
the front of her peacoat.
A raspberry print, hot scab

of bird-dropped fruit. Glow
like the car cigarette lighter
she fingered as a child

thinking orange ring candy.
Or the ponytail sent up
in White Rain and bonfire:

hours with grandmother,
salves, and silent bus rides
to wig shops on Woodward.

She didn't burn, she blew
into flame, combustible
girl known for scarlet nails,

naked legs under a denim
skirt in February. She ran
toward the house lighting

a stand of birches, safflower
finch feeder, the Japanese
maple and patio umbrella

that crumpled like velvet.
For weeks a fireplace smell
in the kitchen. Her Camaro

slow-leaking oil on the drive.
Moths keeping their distance
from a cool harvest moon.

TWO

Loose footing
and a stick in your hand.
At seven you walked
a bear to the edge,
knowing white eyes
meant blind or brain-sick,
sparrows already
landing on its back.

Flushed at the radiator
in a northern bar,
I knew you wanted my
fringed blouse off, sun
on the cliffs of Morrison
and the wild onions
we would scald in fire.

Or instead the boy
at dusk, walking. Red hat
and a burned log cabin,
chimney still standing.
You ordered me the *three
wise men* and its glass
made me grab the table.

How much longer
until you told the story
always growing larger,
bear heavier, raggy fur
like the rug in our motel
lobby. Sometimes you
saw it first, or surprised
as you pissed on the side
of a tree. The shadow

inching, then paw snap
on leaves. I knew you
would die with a gun
and empty room, but then
I counted breaths as you
slept. Michigan a rusty
puddle at the steel works,
your job in a bookstore.
How I would take it
all back if it kept.

Under neon, the ending
changed by day: charge
from the bear, boy
sprinting, spilling. Moon
full, with town dogs
moaning below. The time
you told me a wild fire
chased you both, moment
of boy and bear tumbling

to pine boughs. Nothing
was true but the sound
of men at the pool table,
glass eyes of the heads
mounted above the bar,
my face in the sink. How
the bear fell that night,
ears the size of a boy's
hand, shaking. The pad

of feet on rock, and that
stick you balanced on
at the creek. Not knowing
the size of your frame
at that age, doubled by
night. The scare of your
eyes as rock became ledge,
ledge to claw. The ending
stopped short, your
palm fast at my knee.

MILFOIL & AFTERTHOUGHT

There were four rooms. There were eight. You were in corners and under furniture, near my knees, reflections of your back in stainless steel. Suspenders, Florsheims and avocado linen. There was limestone halfway up, and I knew I'd crash into it if I could move fast. You thought it was a cold place. The light bulbs? It was all like helium to me at that point. I said someone should be taking pictures, the way we were sprawled on the hardwood or propped up on rattan sofas. One time in the airport we were both small and spun together in a leather chair chained to the ceiling. You touched my leg. Nobody was taking pictures, but that doesn't mean it didn't happen, or that we weren't in Frankenmuth five years later, at connecting tables but kept separate. A shed behind the school, or that storm sewer at the dunes, past the grasses, left of concession, the sand that felt like clay, like slip, how blond you had become, I hardly recognized. If you were here in this room you'd remind me of the guitar, the train platform, the silver Cutlass containing me and continuing on past it all. You said we'd go back. I was always a good runner. You said: the smoothest skin ever. We'd seen the skyline from two dozen taxis, our own legs on the bridge, from the grass, from the grass again, in the grass on my front lawn, lit by the cheap plastic solar lamps, from deep past the buoys of Lake Michigan and into the waterways connecting. We knew where we had come from, had that in common. In college I looked out the laundry room window and saw you between leaves, in a corduroy jacket. We're here, you said. There were blue sheets I used instead of curtains. Later I'd be in a hundred rooms with tin ceilings and slim wine glasses, or rectangular tables and cinderblocks and papers. In the subway window I'd look nothing but tired. I would try everything from milk to cactus in hope of turning you to milk and cactus and dark rafters and back again, so when I closed my eyes it was heat and every other color we described. The nights kept us like ants under plastic. I kept you in places that were cool and uncovered. You touched my face like it was years ago and just starting. I was busy fending off letters and drinking green tea and lying in a cool bath. By noon, everything was back where it had been. We're here and we're living, you said.

II.

LOVE ON A TILE FLOOR

VELVET SEASON

A trombone in the yard
or deer at the street sign again
chafing an antler, velvet

in ribbons. Sheets of dry fuzz
old women will boil, strain.
A corrugated box soars by

on the wind, tumbling
then rising. I love it here
in this blanket. Banana

spider hops into the dryer
all legs, and stripped out
with lint he's now woven

into the pattern. Lucky
as a naked girl in tall grass
when planes drift over.

On my gravel drive
a fox drags one ear along
the ground, mite season.

How the starling plucks
up a cigarette dropped,
for a minute smoking

until ash disappears
into wing, tail feathers.
As a child I thought this

burn made the red-winged
blackbird. Barn owl watched,
stuffed and frumpy, dead

mounted in the classroom.
False eyes fallen out, angry,
trailing a boy into the closet.

His delicate chin in the dark.
If the owl had eyes they'd be
through the door, on top

of the kiln with me, ceramic
dust so fine it's in the skin
even after washing. That spring

smell climbs through hair
to scalp, like the thin parade
of ants up a band of sap.

A kite outside when hail
starts falling: wooden frame
split, tail rigged in the trees,

ice bouncing on grass.
Thunderstorm brings us to
the window, to see lightning

touch down in a different yard.
Or ride a metal rod along
the house, energy fanned out

across lawns, up the peeling
birch next door. The shirt
I am wearing crackles.

COPPER HARBOR

Freakish, like a tapestry.
The dark smudge of fish
shanties and smokehouses.
An orange nylon jacket

knotted on the breakwater.
We watched tourists, made
change for their twenties.

The seagulls were quick
as equinox, Evinrude,
flypaper lit with a zippo.

All cabins have the same
linoleum. It's universal.
I took prints with knees
and palms. Read your tale

of botanical swerve, flash
and fragment. Artichoke
or parsnip? The ether surge

of a mower on the parkway
slapped us out of reverie.
I asked you the sound

of fishhook through a lip.
You gave me a silver cup
and claw hammer. I woke

all night inspecting corners,
nasturtiums. Your body
an arrow into the lake.

MAN IN BLUE

Riverside, selling spring peas
and bulbs. Last year's honey
wax candles. The white blouse
off my shoulders, and skin
freckled from weeding, bee
chasing, falling down hills

and off cliffs. Stepping into
skunk dens, then burning
the scent out of my dress.
Selling bracelets I twisted
all winter, foot-shackled
in a sugar beet farmer's shed,
forgetting the mending, milk,

other things with soft names.
I'll show you my finger-lace
bra in the truck stop showers.
Also several flats of petunias
or bunches of chives, purple
flower and hollow green stem.

I don't mind the ants twisting
up my thigh to the smudge
of strawberry jam dripped
there. Thinking of a man
in blue corduroys instead,
bandana around a gash on
his arm. He could bleed

through my sheets, mattress,
and box springs—I wouldn't
get out the hose or whistle
for the dogs. He'd paint both
doors red. Slashes across
the paperwhite narcissus,
blood on sponge cake. Ruby
handprints around my neck.

RAZORBACK

Son of a felon,
his father was famous
for eating through the wall
of a Wisconsin prison.

Seven hours later
his conception
in a Villanova rail car.
It was a year of locusts.

All he knows is clothing:
days with the flat iron
and dry cleaning fluids.
Starch. I tape my hems
straight, and nothing
gets past him.

His father began
by stripping the paint,
selling it in squares,
enjoying the smooth
panic of poison.

What else would drive
a man to fill his belly
with lath and plaster?
He was full for days.
The one thing he gave
his son was hunger,

hands in the fabric,
smoothing the warped
back of my skirt.
But murder, two men
dead in a bathroom.
I want to die on

an afghan, at seventy,
beside two musty
Irish Setters. Not the pin
in the eye, not glass
baked into cheesecake.

How to trust a man
born the night
his father was fished
from the junkyard
lake bottom. Here
in my bed with aloe
on a burned hand.

And his mother
giving birth in a bucket,
a dead man's son,
trees crackling, blood
on the swamp reeds.
She can show him where
to put that empty mouth.

KICKING IT

Fifteen, behind the wheel
on a sugar beet road, black
apples, northeast wind
keeping cold. Your hood
trailing you, or shuffled
with oak leaves, coffee spot
on the calf, ink to fingertips
and center chest (left pocket).

Pack your plastic cowboys
and denim. Wrap the comics
in newspaper or tissue. Drop
twenty pounds overnight,
sink teeth into bed wood
like you mean everything
from here to Tulsa. Baking
your wallet into a rye loaf
only yields half, airspace
and blank sugar spoons.
It's better this way.

The snowy owl pellets
rafters where you dropped
to shifting feed stacks below
(Hot Molly!). Bite your lip
as invitation or accident,
shutting an oven door with
dishrag shoulders. We're up
against a brick alley wall,
drapes swinging, late August
so hardly any clothes to come
off. Like a bee up the sleeve.

A WESTERN

You're on a train, prairie grass
carving to the side. Cow catcher
if only now for grasshoppers.
Quickly, please. Two weeks

since and already I'm driving
my head through the wall,
or in my car, night stabbing.
Rain on my chest, then rats

on twilight runs down the alley
out back. Missing vegetable
scraps, the way your finger
guides a knife. I have never

seen you bleeding. Only once
when there was nothing but
red. Your hands everywhere,
berried like the car you drove

in on. Like Mexico, mother
told me the flowers blew
from a coffin to her window.
Raccoon prints after they drop,

juice marks lingering. Tiny
palm, fingernails, mine with
your skin still under. Poison
berry, you made a fist when

that man touched my arm.
Broke my arm, a doorstep
in Tulsa fifteen years back.
White petals curled and rusty.

The horse in my head told
me riding one day you'd be
on back. No saddle. Horse belly
pinto like a map. Train rails

in stitches that connect us
(accident with a barbed wire
fence). Clutch tightly my pale
hankie when riding through

a field of bees. You know
coming back it will be all
parlors, gas lamps, and doily
under your beer bottle. Hair

I shampooed in the rain,
waiting weeks for it, noon
dropping to cloud, hail to
strike each place you've been.

RED SEA

An afternoon across from you
in copper light. Smuggling

a quart of milk on the city bus
to drink between potholes.

We stood at the edge of a lot
rumbling with maple leaves.

Lie down in it. Lay it down.
An hour later under sixty watt

bulbs, albacore in pepper oil.
Where did I go when your

arm slid across my shoulder?
Even my palms turned cold.

Even gabardine went sharp.
You told a story of cloves sewn

into canvas pillows. A wife
who loved blanched leeks.

A childhood of Appaloosas
that resisted training, or girls

in distant cities wearing silk.
I remembered a chandelier

I once dissected in the basement
without permission. Your face

startled in the stairway. Blood
rides water underground

like another body. Waiting on
a bar stool in Waukegan, knowing

you are in Ashtabula, no phone.
The sound of dancing drifts through.

SNAKESKIN

Let's split. Outside a gray
dog like a mailbox in snow.

Either way I move it's sharp.
Clay, chokeberries, the stoop
at dusk in half shadow.

Your skin is like linoleum
or rolling papers. Where

are your eyes? Next to me
on the train, a man burned
a cross into his forearm.

How many windows in
one town? Flung on the bed

like straight pins, or lovers
who can't quite work it.
They call this sundown.

The only tumbleweed
on our vista: a locust shell

and candy wrapper, stuck
to each other, on the roll.
This is my neck. Please

watch the Haviland. Here,
where tablecloth meets leg

and my sandal upside down.
Knotty pine. Crease behind
knees. Meet me upstairs.

HOUSEWARMING ✓

The city is older than you
know: catalpa trees rough
in your arms, a woman's
gray tabby cat curving into
your hip. Her man at the store,
your breakfast in his hands,
his finger ready to skim
chipped shell from egg whites.

So much attention, and then
you sink into her bath, try
her sage-green towels on your
legs. Nothing telling here,
at least without coaxing. How
you fit. It's your marble foyer.

You chose this emerald
leather furniture. Years later
you wake in a truck driver's
house downriver, next to his son.
An all-night poker game outside
the room. First glass you lift
is tapwater, whiskey, fingernail

slivers of ice left from the night
before. Mascara smudged
from eye to hand, cocktail dress
hiked, stockings missing. Slink
to the toilet, a blanket drawn
over your shoulders, out the back

door. Freight train, and wind
from the double cars, scrap iron.
As a child you always hoped
for hogs instead. Piles of them,
like you heard they went north
to be cut. Wished for a crash

and they'd all run to you, safe,
the most clever animal. Dirt
bikes rust into the chain link
fence. Standing in a halter top,
turquoise jewelry, blood in
the corner of your mouth.

Once you sliced open the vinyl
seats of a Chevette and found
nothing unusual. One time
slammed your hair in a truck
door. It drove away, a button
of your scalp dangling in
the breeze. The broken arm

sawed out of a cast is brand new,
no color, like a cherry ripened
in shade. A man walking by
slows down and hands you his
napkin. Newspapers pause
then skid onto the highway.
A mouse in the milk bottle
so full of drink, can't get out.

FOXGLOVES AT 3 PM

Ballooned on the back porch
like a bullfrog in springtime.
All full of it. The whole world

going down on its neighbor
and then sliding up bus steps
fragrant with Dial, snapping

wintergreen gum. Sunglasses,
duffel bag, nobody knows
how damp your body is.

Rooms the buttercup gold
they use for schools, seen
on desks, hushed in cotton.

What's not a hustle? No
need for silk when you've
got grease. At the opening

reception, nobody checked
the broom closet for nudes.
There were hours pressing

faces under the paintings,
a glass of whole milk split
between us before stained

glass grottoes. Grandparents
dressed you in lederhosen
every autumn. I was lost

as a child and felt my way
into a neighboring borough.
Why were we the only two

left at the end of the song?
It sounded like shaking, coal
dust, bells, a sitar and tabla

set loose in the wet mines.
We used to meet at the back
table, like we were corporate.

You would help me with my
buttons. I walked that room
and stepped through the blinds

into midday traffic, our haze
a secret. Each dress I snagged
on the same broken hinges.

GIRL IN CHAIR

The streets sew themselves
a beaded mat you can buy
every night. Catfish in bed
with the rushes. Everything
sleeping deep together.

Needlepoint is half blood
most of the time. You miss
once, twice, by the window.
How else to stitch flowers,
or the red mailbox waiting
for a postman's blue vest.

All a game of in and out.
Blood waiting to dump
its oxygen, the mosquito
and waxwing, storm fronts
quaking above as moths.

A seam-ripper hacks
the work in seconds, string
cut to a quarter. Your love
is the one sunk, midnight
in the Monongahela. How
did you not wake when
the river broke like a pane?

A page slits your fingertip
but you keep turning. Now
the cicadas start their fall
from tree to lawn. Cherry
blossoms ride the gutters.
Lightning on the air, men
chasing their hats home.

FERNS

Step into my pantry,
down the stairs into ankle
deep leaves. Fronds

bulge in your pockets
like lipstick. Skirts are for
girls. We're older

and sleepless eight
years since. We both cut
our hair at thirty,

traded the rivets
and magazines for tempura.
The nights of wax.

Butter pressed in
the shape of a lamb, clown.
Pencil sketches

of our bodies dredged
from the botanical garden
pond. Deer watching.

The slim bronze pair
they'd erect in memoriam.
That cool summer

we carried glass
tumblers everywhere, like
scapulae. Remember

our tan lines, field
glasses. Contact dermatitis.
Asleep in the reeds

without a basket.
Follow my porch rails in
autumn darkness.

How they feel under
hands: coverlet, egg white,
kerosene, ultraviolet.

FISH IN WINTER

Your body at the window,
my body, Zilwaukee
bridge in the distance,
sunrise, pipes shimmering
with freeze in the basement.

I will warm your flask
in my hands this morning,
lick whiskey from the cap
before twisting. All this
at your slow step from bed

and hand on my neck
as I wash my face in a soup
bowl. Thinking the fish
are pears in yarn blankets,
the heavy sweet of honey

dropped into your tea.
The whole sport like love
on a tile floor. Your Rambler
rolled out on the ice, depth
finder and auger, boom

and crack from below.
I wrap you an egg on wheat,
cigarettes to pass, sausage
from duck season. Scent
of my shoulder in your beard.

One year you chased me
onto the ice, or did you
follow me, testing how
much the river could take.
You said fish hung drowsy

at the weedline, suspended
where water is warmest.
I thought of a bathtub
on a January morning, hiss
of the teapot, burning toes.

We will bake the fish
in paper, with orange juice
as I rub oil on your fingers,
watch your back at the fire,
face deep in the heat.

III.

THE WAY OF THE HAND

THE TWINS

I see it: no more dusk
to your days. Months ago we
stood on a porch loaded with
empty terracotta pots.

Matchbooks, snowbound
floribunda, empty rice sacks.
It occurs to me that everything
is still there without us,

creaking with temperature
swings and rainstorms. Smoke
from the three women next door,
locked out and waiting.

There were landscapes
in acrylic. Chimes from clocks
we couldn't find. Plum tomatoes
in quart baskets. I watched

them shiver into pools
on the countertop, as if you
had rolled them in your hands
for hours. Light was gold

and inching closer, taxis
banked cheek to cheek on
the highway below. Evenings
like this I wanted kept

on ice or tucked beneath
a layer of silk. I didn't have silk,
only wool and nylon. There was
nothing left of the night,

only train cars and breath.
They could dust me for prints
and find just fingertip salt and rust.
You were a halo of consonants

in the dull ebb of my pulse.
I could have hung my jacket up.
You could have told me how
they found us and took us

to our opposite corners, separate
lawns, rooms where we both slept on
twin beds, star quilts, lost in the scent
of cotton batting and blackjack gum.

BRICK DUST

Whispers between rooms,
or not. Just the sock basket
midair, swinging from pins
and embroidery floss. Was

there a river? Are we still
under two layers of raw blue
flannel, reading instead of
the obvious? Someone told

me that flour on the calves
is a sign of missed chances.
But what about Wednesday
morning, in the hall under

Boykin, your corduroy to
my cinderblock, shuttle bus
idling in the bay. They now
call blankets *warming* instead

of *electric*. You might find
me in a bathtub full of chalk
and glycerin one day, asleep.
Why not say we planned it?

There's a church of cat hair
and thread under our table.
Go deliver your slides, sign
all of the desk rosters, stall

the service elevator for two
minutes against the garbage
and button-pressers. I'll be
in the corner, like fifth grade

only meaner. Tapioca, resin,
steel wool. My back against
a screen door. The damp tang
of mercurochrome and nettles.

COMMONLAW

Our midnight shampoos
and haircuts, nights
ending in bookstores,

collapsed on parkas
like camping out
for a Greyhound
ten years ago.

Knife in your pocket.
Wearing my socks,
scarf, and knowing
I'd wake Saturday

after your plane lifted
West. No coffee there.
Rooms all spinning
and heated. Moths,

some big as blue jays
rattling my windows
three months later.
All that wing dust.

I'm out of aloe
from rugburn, gnats
and smashed apples.
Lead me to the barn

and pen me. Forget
how hard it is trapping
minnows in a hookah.
You have to run

from your own owls.
If you fall through
a snowy creek bed,
hit your ear on bramble

and land balls-up
don't sue the landlord.
I'll still take you.

DRIVING AWAY FROM YOUR BODY

They arrested us for fighting in the street
like two footballers on rival teams, wet

from the showers, or was it German beer
dribbled down our polyester sweaters

that started everything, shoving and bar
stools brandished like stilettos or mace

or a shot of tequila to the left eye, acrylic
nails raking an earlobe. Years later, back

in that neighborhood, there were lights
finally, and no evidence of the damage

we'd inflicted like dueling renegades
with bandanas and pistols stuffed down

our dungarees. In a chance meeting
we would be strung to each other like

the dream catchers that my grandmother
made after they took all of her needles.

We were both the woof and the weave
all in one, only hovering over a can

of Sterno and surrounded by shredded
credit card statements and newspapers.

I stalked you in the cool sarcophagus
of payphones and bank vestibules.

You rubbed graphite on my notepads
to see what lists I had written, took

the ribeyes from my freezer. We were
crocodile and zebra and a drought filled

with locusts and laser-guided missles.
The mornings after our nights left us

begging for salve and Canadian
bacon and ice for the bruising.

I was a Latin King to your Gangster
Disciple, straddling the dotted line

between your side of California
Avenue and mine. We argued that

the best way to settle our differences
involved nudity and a room filled

with the soft mozzarella we once
bought at a deli in Newark, nursing

ourselves back from three days fishing
on a speedboat that was not loaded

with dynamite, which we eventually
regretted as the sunsets blinded us,

Chianti settled into our stomachs, gulls
circling as if they knew something.

LUNAR ECLIPSE

Starboard, the red-wing
blackbirds all that are left.
In the cattails, I think —
between scratches — of helping
you out of the most vicious
wool sweater. The places
it got you the worst, neck pink
like a ruffle. It's a night of sky
closings, like that store
on my street, windows blacked
then scraped clear each season.

Did you scuff onto anything
in my house? The teacups,
Rose of Sharon, the ledge
that nailed your forehead
like a bat. That knife
you used to slice a pear.
My finger on your eyebrow.

Standing in the mud, it feels
cold fills you. To the waist,
nowhere to gaze but up,
like when you found the bees
nest in a gutter. Back when
I read your stings like braille.
And in the spa, how I paid
hundreds to be wrapped
in dirty cloths. So much
left at the end of the world.
My face sunk to bone
and you at my table.

THE OLD NEIGHBORHOOD

They must have been so young
when they burned the house to the ground
and left with their suitcases at dawn,

two Brooklynites incognito as swordfish
in the Mississippi. There were no trees left
on that street, only pillowcase outlines

in the windows, occasional bees descending
from rooftop sunflowers. What did she pack
instead of burning? The hat collection left

drenched in bacon grease and weak kerosene.
Books and leaflets she lit with a flaming
chestnut, held out in tongs. His beloved

pipe stuffed with crepe and lit on the sofa.
Another evening of crossword puzzles,
a roast and rolls, the cling of her powdered

blouse, arms elbow-high in rubber dish gloves
and Palmolive. He was the one who strayed
past the curtain that divided bedroom

from kitchen, a newspaper collapsing fast
into its folds, sparking her favorite lamp's fringe.
Men in movies did this with a flourish,

but they were torching the villain's humble squat
or a town ghosted over with the fever, brothels
gone dishonest and beyond recover.

Who knows how they escaped that night,
stumbled to the alley with loud pockets and jaunty
steps, so many changes of clothes layered

like vagabond paper dolls caught mid-tramp.
He held her elbow as they collapsed
into a taxi, bought her coffee at the train station

between the lost and the waiting. The sulfur
lingered in her fingertips, tucked like wrens in
a wool shawl, one silk daisy pinned at her throat.

IT'S ALL TOO MUCH

He was too sick to shuffle down to the VFW Hall for cold, cheap beer. She was too awake to put on a fox fur vest and rouge from a snuff box. The alleys were too perpendicular to the roads, so the runoff went north. When the ossified creams and lead feather whisks hovered above her bed at night, he was there too: all peacock and cormorant, so peregrine he vanished from sight when the busses heaved through an intersection. And the wheat germ strewn on the windowsill? Precaution. Some days her words would be used against her, like salmonella. He was too rough in the head to shuttle the pennies into their paper sleeves, preferring pockets. She walked thirty blocks west before finding the river moved. He was too occupied by minutiae like Avogadro and the depth of tar. She marinated a brisket in South African pinotage plus a box of cloves. It's a mean sky. In minutes it will make you turn back over yourself. It's shifty. She remembers when a shift was always a dress meant to be lifted over face and shoulders silhouetted in front of a window. His shifts were always noted by the blue penmanship of a time clock. His idea of hand cream was tallow and peppermint. Bee balm. Pumice. She was all under his hands like milk from a faucet. He got so lost one winter in the woods that he rebuilt everything, burned it down all over. His hands were all over her body. She cried at the sight of salvia or rue in a container garden under a remote control awning. Is it true they both looked forward to funerals, for the whisky? Did they ever wander past the monument at the same time, separately? He learned the ridge of her neckline was the best place to remember months in the service overseas. Or the underside of a rowboat. The vulnerable, white belly of a catfish.

MANISTEE

Took the river with you.

Left fingerprints in window
soot, a brush of skin-oil
on the wall. Cello curve

of hip and beltway around
your middle. Where I'd cut
to make half-and-half,

decisions of what to keep,
or to snap the shutters
and brass hinges to both.

My face was the color
of tinned flan, reflective dun
scarred in moisture, shaking.

I opened my mouth and wine
crashed to the linoleum
in green glass shatters.

Like we were so hungry
we sucked each other's fingers
for something. Or midnights

in the grocery. You must have
been mostly salt, because it was
everywhere, in and out of water.

Once you hid my clothes
and we stood naked in the fog,
Canada geese dabbling

by the rocks, my stomach tight
from the potato you burned for me.
The blanket suddenly all briar

and beetle until we rolled out
into the grass. Afterwards
the relief sketch of a swimmer

my back imprinted in blades.
A different afternoon, somewhere
else, later. The blankets fell one

by one to the floor and the echo
woke you. Like two pigeons
colliding on the roof. I was on

your stomach. Both of our faces
turned to the window. Sheers
billowed away from the sill

like a princess half sun
half diesel exhaust. Wading
into shallows, then sleeping

our way through it. I knew
each vein in your neck
and where it went.

BIRD OF DANGER

Bone shoulder
in a string dress.
How I would sing
my blues in your ear
each morning, bees
at the window,

no one thinking
other than honey.
Always different
from above. Nest still
until the wasp-smoker,
paper cells flapping,
wing upon wing.

Hawk took the scrap
lot overnight, Ohio
vaudeville store fronts
now paint shops, a bar
where I ate my half
of our dinner. Like
field and mouse,

tail like string to kite.
I would follow you
with all my ribbons
lifting in wind. Light
on an interstate
in autumn, the soy

plot with vultures
necking a stiff raccoon.
Who farmed around
the barn fallen-in
or lived in the shingled
house? Childhood

birds drawn in air
like a team of buttocks
on the swoop. You
have me at an angle
on the bed, as crows
turn the road to ocean,

monarchs cresting into
the headlights. A Cessna
cracks our sleep, how
pale your face is before
eyes open. Please don't
tip the finch nest

from the ceiling, broom
in hand. When a sparrow
leaps to the table
offer a grain of rice,
your finger to sit.

ROYAL BLUE

We were two strands of thread
snagged on a wooden barn door.
You were odd granite shrapnel

in my safety goggles. One wet
sheep standing on the driveway.
A bad stomachache after apples

and capers. If I painted the wall
ecru, you walked into it bloody
handed. Those days were less

Flemish and more Portuguese,
at least in the beginning. What
Old Master would've measured

from my elbow to the toaster?
If oxen crowded the interstate
we were in no way responsible

or even aware. I was not your
wife, not even close. Alpacas
always left me shivering like

a tuberculosis stick, or elevator
skipping a floor. A cartoon man
naked in a barrel can never be

unrolled. I ironed handkerchiefs
for quick cash. I let them weld
me behind some mesh. It's mean

the way we flush right out, like
milk, and then we begin all over.
Once, we both lived underwater.

COYOTE

You called me *hellcat*
like I was nothing
but trouble.

You said I could melt
bricks if I wanted.
I chose you over
all other disturbances.

How gently you shaved
my leg when I let you.
I would boil water
all day without knowing.

You taught me to make
a meal out of snow.
The *one-two, one-two*
of my upstairs neighbors,

sand in your pockets.
And I have forgotten
what went between
and everything after.

But to nip your wrist
again on the rooftop
of St. Aloysius.
For this I would trade

my coat in winter.
Knot my hair and hang
until the wind took me.
All of this was fiction.

The sum of our bodies
is always uncertain,
and the timber wolf
pacing your parking lot

vanished every morning
before I woke. We are
resting comfortably now:
you flushed in a room

of hands, and I empty
with my back to plaster.
So long to the crickets
that crouched in each

motel room corner.
Goodbye to the arm
I bit off, left in your bed.

BIRD BONES

Empty me. It's autumn
and we're still here
in the pink of it.

Who said anything
about marabou, hair
rinsed in rainwater and ale.

I'm better in trees.
You won't have to search
for nipples in my shirt

once it's November.
I'll put it out there. Canada
geese wander into the yard

like they're reading
my meter. I don't mind
the company. Boys next

door shadow the thicket
for a glimpse, as a pheasant
skitters onto the clothes line

and away with my garters.
Why the red, and not tangerine?
If you lived here I'd never

get dressed. Serious trouble
when shopping, lawn mowing.
More practical in Florida.

You can bend my arms
any direction without a snap.
Follow the muscles of my back

in your Buick, like that might
bring you deep northwoods
fast as gunfire. Your wolf dog

sleeps best at my feet. You're in
these sheets, oak and willow,
match that sets a house burning.

SLIM

The nude, then the crease
in the sheets when she stood.
Or a bather on the day
fish slid sideways to the coast
and covered it all. Neckline,
a thin hint of bone.

One song two men
played different ways, wax
to waxwing, the landlady
with newspaper and vinegar
at the window. Soft cloth
or a press of print
in the very corner, over
a red speck of moon.

Who owned that room
or the song that taught
the way of the hand, how
quickly we learned it.
This is when you stop
or where, as spiders kept
knitting in the doorframe

of the antique dealer's shop.
It was a toss between
the china plate—how you
wanted to douse it with thick
wine and sage—or the likeness
of your hog's-head girl, down
in the mouth, nickel plate
on a forties cigar case.

And what you kept in it
or would have. Your studies
in charcoal: fancy carp in still
pond. Two sheets of one song.
Dust hung to the rafters,
a crack in the door panes
and what it made of us.

ABOUT THE AUTHOR

Mary Biddinger is an Assistant Professor of English at The University of Akron, where she serves on faculty of the Northeast Ohio Master of Fine Arts program, teaching creative writing and literature. She has an MFA from Bowling Green State University, and a Ph.D. from the University of Illinois at Chicago. Her poems have appeared in ACM, *American Literary Review*, *Crazyhorse*, *The Iowa Review*, *Ploughshares*, and many other journals. She is an Associate Editor of the literary magazine RHINO.

bodily knowledge
cognate
overlay

clothes
food
animals

Printed in the United States
72111LV00002B/40-105